Eureka!
I Found Them

The No Longer Lost Dessert Recipes

MICHELLE GUSSOW

authorHOUSE®

AuthorHouse™
1663 Liberty Drive
Bloomington, IN 47403
www.authorhouse.com
Phone: 1 (800) 839-8640

Published by AuthorHouse 04/04/2019

ISBN: 978-1-7283-0716-9 (sc)
ISBN: 978-1-7283-0715-2 (e)

Special thanks to my friends on social media for the AS&J flavor ideas.: Valerie Lynne Smith, Ellen L. Zamecnik, Fiona McInerney, Ann Rose, Helen Ann Reeves and Louise Ann Blizzard Though, I did not use all the suggestions I appreciated all of them equally. Thanks to Clare Juland for coming up with the name Amnesty Bars. Thank you also to Marianne Carter, Deborah Toquato, Regina Keim, and Dan Ker for joining in the thread.

Table of Contents

A FISTFUL OF RECIPES

VEGAN, GLUTEN FREE

CAVALCADE OF CANDY

Foreword

In 2003 when I cobbled together my first dessert recipe book "Just Desserts" I had two folders, regular ratty pocket folders like you would buy at the school book store, filled with loose pages of hand written recipes and notes. I also had separate pages that listed the recipes found in the folders. Before sitting down at the computer to enter "Just Desserts" into a word processing file one of the folders disappeared...along with the list of what was contained in that folder. Unfazed I created my little book from the folder at hand, printed the pages and took the whole mess to a local printing business where they did their version of binding.

In 2018 I ventured to create a better version of a dessert recipe book using recipes from "Just Desserts" as well as some not previously used from the folder that had not vanished into the blue. A few days after I had "The Great Schmoogle Dessert Book" in my hands I found my missing list and was able to recreate at least most of the items. There was never a doubt that I would do another recipe book and after toying with a few different titles I decided the most natural was my reaction when I located the elusive list. "Eureka! I found them!"

CAKES AND PIES

Many of these recipes start with boxed cake mix to make things easier for you.

Chocolate Frosting Bomb
For frosting lovers

1 box yellow cake mix
Ingredients needed to prepare cake mix
2 16 oz. tubs ready to spread chocolate frosting

Prepare cake mix as directed on box. Pour into greased and floured bundt pan and bake according to directions. Cool partially in pan. Turn out to continue cooling. Turn cake upside down. Cut a 1 inch thick slice off the bottom of the cake and set aside. Scoop out cake to make a "ditch" approximately 2" wide and 2" deep. Soften frosting from one tub by microwaving for 20 seconds. Fill the "ditch" with the frosting. Replace the bottom of the cake and allow to rest for about an hour. Turn cake upright. Soften remaining chocolate frosting and spread over the cake. If desired decorate with crumbs made from the removed cake. Allow to stand until frosting is set. Enjoy!

Chocolate Frosting Roll
Another for frosting lovers

5 egg yolks
½ cup granulated sugar
4 tablespoons sifted flour
5 egg whites
2 16 oz. tubs ready to spread chocolate frosting

Grease a jelly roll pan. Line with wax paper. Grease again. Preheat oven to 400 degrees. Beat the egg yolks and 5 tablespoons of the sugar until light in color. Add the flour. Mix well. Beat the egg whites until stiff but not dry. Fold into the egg yolk mixture. Spread mixture into prepared jelly roll pan Bake for 12 minutes or until tester comes out clean. Sprinkle remaining sugar on sheet of wax paper. Turn cake out onto wax paper. Remove wax paper it had been baked on. Roll cake to cool. Unroll cake. Spread generously with chocolate frosting and roll cake tight. Cover with frosting. (you may or may not use all frosting) Enjoy!

Cherry Cordial Cupcakes

1 box classic white cake mix
Ingredients needed to prepare cake mix
1 8-10 oz. jar maraschino cherries, drained
2 cups semisweet chocolate morsels

Prepare cake mix as directed using the egg whites only option. Spoon batter into mini muffin tin cups filling each 3/4 full. Place a maraschino cherry in the center of the batter in each cup pushing down just slightly. (cherry should still be visible) Bake as directed. Cool cupcakes completely. Melt semisweet morsels using your preferred method. Dip cooled cupcakes in melted chocolate and let stand on wax paper until coating is set. You may refrigerate to speed up this process. Enjoy!

Ebony and Ivory Cake

1 box classic white cake mix

Ingredients needed to prepare using egg whites only method

2 teaspoons all purpose flour

Black food coloring GEL

Anise extract

White frosting to cover layer cake

Black licorice pieces (optional)

Preheat oven according to directions on box. Prepare two nine inch layer cake pans and prepare cake mix according to box directions. Reserve one cup of batter. Pour remaining batter into the two pans. Add 2 teaspoons flour, black food coloring gel (eyeball this to get desired darkness) and 2 drops anise extract to the reserved batter. (this can be a very strong flavor so you may wish to taste test the batter for what you prefer. You may adjust according to taste by adding more or using less) Mix well. Scoop one half of black batter over batter in each pan and swirl to create a marble effect. Bake as directed. Cool. Assemble and frost cake. You may add anise to the frosting if desired. Use licorice pieces to garnish the top of cake. Enjoy!

Mandlen Naches Cake

Mandlen is Yiddish for Almonds. Naches (pronounced like the "ach" in achtung) is Joy.

1 box classic white cake mix

Ingredients as needed to prepare cake mix using egg whites only method

1 16 oz. tub vanilla frosting

1 16 oz. tub chocolate frosting

2 cups slivered almonds

2 cups shredded coconut

Prepare batter as directed. Stir in 1½ cups of the shredded coconut. Pour batter into two 9" round cake pans and bake according to directions. Cool. To assemble spread bottom layer with vanilla frosting. (you will have left over frosting) Top vanilla frosting with the remaining coconut. Cover with second layer of cake. Frost sides and top with chocolate frosting. Press slivered almonds into top and sides of cake. Enjoy!

Streusel Filled Cottage Cheese Cake

Cake:

1 box classic white cake mix

2 cups full fat small curd cottage cheese

4 egg whites

Water

Powdered sugar

Crumble:

½ cup (1 stick butter, softened)

2 ¼ cups all purpose flour

1 cup firmly packed dark brown sugar

2 teaspoons cinnamon

½ cup finely chopped walnuts

Preheat oven according to cake mix box directions. Grease and flour a bundt pan. Combine cake mix, cottage cheese and egg whites mixing well. If batter is too stiff add water one tablespoon at a time until desired consistancy. Pour half of the batter into prepared pan. Top with the cinnamon crumble. Pour remaining batter over the crumble. Bake according the box directions. Cool for fifteen minutes in pan. Turn out and cool completely. Dust with powdered sugar. Enjoy!

To make crumble cut the butter into the flour. Mix in the remaining ingredients.

Hanukkah Apple Cinnamon Cake

1 vanilla cake mix

Ingredients needed to prepare cake mix

1 heaping teaspoon cinnamon

2 small granny smith apples, peeled, cored, chopped

1 cup chopped walnuts

½ cup white frosting

¼ teaspoon cinnamon

Prepare batter according to package directions using ¼ cup less water than indicated. Add cinnamon and blend well. Stir in apples and nuts. Pour into a bundt pan which has been prepared according to package directions. Bake according to package directions. Cool 15 minutes. Invert on to a plate and allow to finish cooling completely. Soften frosting in microwave until it is pourable but not too runny. Stir in cinnamon and drizzle over the top of the cake. Enjoy!

Peanut Butter and Jelly Tea Cakes

2 ½ cups all-purpose flour

1 2/3 cups sugar

3 ½ teaspoons baking powder

1 teaspoon salt

¾ cup milk

2/3 cup shortening

3 eggs

½ cup milk

2 teaspoons vanilla extract

Creamy peanut butter

Grape or strawberry jam

Powdered sugar

Preheat oven to 350 degrees. Combine dry ingredients.

Stir in ¾ cup milk and shortening. Beat at medium speed for 2 minutes. Add remaining ingredients except for the peanut butter and jelly. Beat another 2 minutes. Pour batter into two 15 x 10-inch baking sheets. Bake for 20 minutes or until tester comes out clean. Cool completely. Spread one cake with a layer of peanut butter. (soften in microwave if necessary for easy spreading) Spread jam on second cake and turn over onto first cake. Dust generously with powdered sugar. Cut into squares. Enjoy!

Cream Cheese Pie

Pie crust:

½ cup (1 stick) margarine (do not substitute butter)

1 cup all purpose flour

Filling:

24 oz. full fat cream cheese

1 small box instant vanilla pudding mix (4 serving size)

2 cups whipping cream

½ cup granulated sugar

Preheat oven to 375 degrees. Combine margarine and flour to form dough. Roll out to 1/8 inch thickness and place in nine inch pie pan. Flute edge as desired. Use beans or pie weights to fill for the baking process. Bake for 20 minutes. Remove from oven and remove the weights. Return to oven for another 15 minutes or until golden all over. Cool completely.

Blend cream cheese and pudding mix. In a larger bowl beat cream and sugar until soft peaks form. Fold into cream cheese mixture. Pour into prepared crust. Chill until set. If desired top with fruit to serve. Enjoy!

Note: This recipe is not intended to produce a very sweet product.

Chocolate Chip Pudding Pie

Crust:

1 ¼ cups chocolate cookie crumbs

1/3 cup margarine, melted

Combine ingredients and press onto bottom and sides of 8 or 9 inch pie pan. Bake at 425 degrees for 10 minutes. Set aside to cool.

Filling:

2 boxes chocolate instant pudding and pie filling (5.9 oz. size)

4 cups cold milk

1 package mini semisweet chocolate morsels (reserve 1/2 cup of morsels)

Whipped topping (whichever you prefer)

Prepare pudding mix as directed. If there are different directions for preparing pudding and pie filling follow the directions for making pudding. Stir in the morsels not in reserve. Spoon into pie shell and refrigerate for 1 hour. Cover with whipped topping and sprinkle with reserved semisweet morsels. Enjoy!

Trouble Pie

1 ¼ cups crumbs made from chocolate sandwich cookies

1/3 cup melted margarine

2 8 oz jars fudge ice cream topping

1 quart vanilla ice cream, softened

1 cup chopped peanuts (not dry roasted)

½ cup whole peanuts (not dry roasted)

Combine sandwich cookie crumbs and margarine. Press onto bottom and sides of a 9- inch pie pan. Bake at 425 degrees for 10 minutes. Cool. Heat fudge topping so it is pourable. Pour 1/3 of the topping onto the bottom of the pie shell. Sprinkle with ½ cup of the chopped peanuts. Cover with ½ of the ice cream. Freeze until set. Repeat process once. Cover top with remaining fudge and whole peanuts. Enjoy!

Cashew Pie

Crust:

1 cup all purpose flour

½ cup margarine

Cut margarine into the flour and combine to form dough. Roll out to 1/8 inch thick and line a 9" pie pan with the dough. Score the bottom several times with a fork. Flute as desired. Set aside.

Filling:

3 eggs, beaten

1 cup granulated sugar

1 cup light corn syrup

1 teaspoon vanilla extract

2 cups chopped cashew nuts

Preheat oven to 300 degrees. Blend all ingredients except for the cashews. Stir in cashews. Pour into prepared dough. Bake at 300 degrees for 1 hour or until tester comes out clean. Cool. Enjoy!

Story Break

It's All About the Frosting

Actually, to be more specific it's all about the chocolate frosting. As far back as I can remember I did not care what kind of cake was served as long as there was chocolate frosting on it. Okay, maybe not a great idea to put chocolate frosting on lemon or carrot cake.

I have always had a hierarchy when it came to being served cake. My most favorite was chocolate cake with chocolate frosting. Coming in second: white or yellow cake with chocolate frosting, third: chocolate cake with frosting that wasn't chocolate. Last on the list was any cake that wasn't chocolate with any frosting that wasn't chocolate. Okay, I get it I should have just appreciated getting to have some cake. But that being said admit it. You, too, have your hierarchy in the cake department and you know that you were disappointed at least somewhat if it wasn't your favorite...especially if it was your own birthday cake.

The bakery where we got our special occasion cakes only did white frosting when you ordered chocolate cake. I supposed it could have been special ordered but no one ever thought of it. Nobody seemed to understand that I would have far preferred to have white cake if it meant that I could have chocolate frosting. I adored that bakery's cupcakes as they sold chocolate cupcakes with a mound of chocolate frosting. I would always eat the cake part first and eat the frosting last, by itself. Yes, I loved it that much.

I loved the chocolate frosting so much that, yes, I am someone who can sit down with a tub of ready to spread frosting and just eat it with a spoon. Most people have told me I was nuts for doing this....Hmmm, nuts mixed with chocolate frosting. You know, that's actually not a bad idea.

BARS AND COOKIES

Chocolate Chip Toffee Peanut Butter Cookies

½ cup shortening

½ cup sugar

½ cup packed dark brown sugar

½ teaspoon salt

1 egg

½ cup natural peanut butter (no sugar added)

1 ¼ cups sifted flour

½ teaspoon baking soda

¾ cup semisweet chocolate morsels*

¾ cup toffee bits

Cream together the shortening and the sugars. Add salt, egg, and peanut butter blending well. Combine the flour and baking soda. Add to sugar mixture. Blend. Stir in semisweet morsels and toffee bits Form dough into walnut size balls. Place balls on a cookie sheet. Bake at 375 degrees for 7 to 10 minutes. Cool. Enjoy!

*if you prefer you can substitute milk chocolate chips

Fantasy Chocolate Bars

1 cup margarine, softened

2/3 cup sugar

2/3 cup dark brown sugar

2 eggs

1 teaspoon vanilla

2 cups flour

¾ cup cocoa

1 teaspoon baking soda

½ teaspoon salt

2 cups semisweet chocolate morsels

1 16 oz. tub ready to spread chocolate frosting

Preheat oven to 350 degrees.

Cream margarine and sugars. Add the eggs and vanilla. Beat 2 minutes at medium speed. Combine flour, cocoa, baking soda, and salt. Blend into creamed mixture. Stir in semisweet morsels. Spread mixture into greased 15 x10-inch baking sheet. Bake for 20 minutes or until tester comes out clean. Cool. Use handle of a wooden spoon to poke holes in the pan cookie at 2 inch intervals. Do not poke all the way through. Place tub of frosting in microwave for 20 to 25 seconds until it becomes pourable but not too liquid. Pour over top of pan cookie making sure to get it into the poked holes. Let stand until set. You can speed the process by putting in the refrigerator. Cut into squares or rectangles. Enjoy!

Indecision Bars

2 ¼ cups all-purpose flour

1 teaspoon baking soda

1 teaspoon salt

1 cup margarine, softened

¾ cup granulated sugar

¾ cup firmly packed dark brown sugar

1 teaspoon vanilla extract

2 large eggs

¾ cup milk chocolate morsels

¾ cup semi sweet chocolate morsels

¾ cup white (vanilla) baking morsels

Optional: ½ cup chopped walnuts or other nuts

Preheat oven to 350 degrees. Combine flour, baking soda and salt in small bowl. Beat margarine, granulated sugar, brown sugar and vanilla extract in large mixer bowl until creamy. Add eggs, one at a time, beating well after each addition. Gradually beat in flour mixture. Stir in morsels and nuts. Grease a 15 x 10-inch baking sheet. Spread dough into prepared pan. Bake for 20 to 25 minutes or until golden brown. Cool slightly. Cut and continue cooling. Enjoy!

Kitchen Sink Bars

1 cup margarine, softened

2/3 cup sugar

2/3 cup dark brown sugar

2 eggs

1 teaspoon vanilla

2 cups flour

¾ cup cocoa

1 teaspoon baking soda

½ teaspoon salt

½ cup semi sweet chocolate morsels

½ cup milk chocolate morsels

1/2 cup white baking morsels

¼ finely chopped walnuts

¼ cup finely chopped almonds

Preheat oven to 350 degrees.

Cream margarine and sugars. Add the eggs and vanilla. Beat
2 minutes at medium speed. Combine flour, cocoa, baking

soda, and salt. Blend into creamed mixture. Add morsels and nuts. Mix thoroughly. Spread mixture into greased 15 x 10-inch baking sheet. Bake for 20 minutes or until tester comes out clean. Enjoy!

Mint Chocolate Chip Bars

1 ½ cups all purpose flour

½ teaspoon baking powder

¼ teaspoon salt

2 eggs

2 tablespoon water

1 teaspoon vanilla extract

¼ teaspoon peppermint extract (use more if you like it stronger)

6 oz. white baking chocolate (might be called white coating)

1/3 cup butter, melted and cooled

green food coloring

1 cup mini semisweet chocolate morsels

Preheat oven to 350 degrees. Combine flour, baking powder and salt. Add sugar, eggs, water and extracts. Mix well. Using your preferred method melt white baking chocolate. Add along with melted butter to batter and mix well. Add green food coloring one drop at a time until desired shade of green is reached. (this is personal preference) Stir in semisweet morsels. Pour batter into 9 x 13 baking pan which has been lightly greased or use a food release spray. Bake for 20 to 25 minutes or until tester comes out clean. Cool. Cut into bars. Enjoy!

Rocky Road Bars

1 cup margarine, softened

2/3 cup sugar

2/3 cup dark brown sugar

2 eggs

1 teaspoon vanilla

2 cups flour

¾ cup cocoa

1 teaspoon baking soda

½ teaspoon salt

1 cup mini semi sweet baking chips

1 cup chopped walnuts

4 cups mini marshmallows

Preheat oven to 350 degrees.

Cream margarine and sugars. Add the eggs and vanilla. Beat 2 minutes at medium speed. Combine flour, cocoa, baking soda, and salt. Blend into creamed mixture. Stir in mini chips and walnuts. Spread mixture into greased 15 x 10-inch baking sheet. Bake for 20 minutes or until tester comes out clean. Pour mini marshmallows over the top and return to oven. Leave in just until marshmallows begin to brown. Cool. Enjoy!

Striped Chocolate Chip Coconut Cookies

½ cup shortening

½ cup sugar

1 egg separated

1 teaspoon vanilla

¾ cup flour

¼ teaspoon salt

¼ teaspoon baking powder

2/3 cup shredded coconut

½ cup mini semisweet chocolate morsels

Remaining morsels from package

Preheat oven to 375 degrees

Cream together the shortening and sugar. Beat in the egg yolk and vanilla. Mix in the flour, salt and baking powder. Stir in ½ cup mini morsels Beat egg white until just frothy. Roll dough into walnut size balls. Dip into egg white, then roll in coconut. Place on greased baking sheet. Flatten slightly. Bake for 8 to 9 minutes until coconut just begins to brown. Cool completely. Using your preferred method melt the remaining semisweet morsels. Use a spoon to drizzle chocolate stripes on the cool cookies. Allow to set. Enjoy!

Aloha Bars

2 ¼ cups all-purpose flour

1 teaspoon baking soda

1 teaspoon salt

1 cup margarine, softened

¾ cup granulated sugar

¾ cup firmly packed light brown sugar

1 teaspoon vanilla extract

2 large eggs

¾ cup finely chopped macadamia nuts

1 cup shredded coconut (I usually used the unsweetened but if you prefer a sweeter bar the sweetened works well)

Preheat oven to 350 degrees. Combine flour, baking soda and salt in small bowl. Beat margarine, granulated sugar, brown sugar, vanilla extract in large mixer bowl until creamy. Add eggs, one at a time, beating well after each addition. Gradually beat in flour mixture. Stir in nuts and coconut. Grease a 15 x 10-inch baking sheet. Spread dough into prepared pan. Bake for 20 to 25 minutes or until golden brown. Cool slightly. Cut and continue cooling. Enjoy!

Happy Trails Bars

2 ¼ cups all-purpose flour

1 teaspoon baking soda

1 teaspoon salt

1 cup margarine, softened

¾ cup granulated sugar

¾ cup firmly packed dark brown sugar

1 teaspoon vanilla extract

2 large eggs

1 cup coarsely chopped nuts (feel free to use your favorites)

1 cup dried fruit (again feel free to use any of your favorites)

Preheat oven to 350 degrees. Combine flour, baking soda and salt in small bowl. Beat margarine, granulated sugar, brown sugar, vanilla extract in large mixer bowl until creamy. Add eggs, one at a time, beating well after each addition. Gradually beat in flour mixture. Stir in dried fruit and nuts. Grease a 15 x 10-inch baking sheet. Spread dough into prepared pan. Bake for 20 to 25 minutes or until golden brown. Cool slightly. Cut and continue cooling. Enjoy!

Mixed Bag Bars

2 ¼ cups all-purpose flour

1 teaspoon baking soda

1 teaspoon salt

1 cup margarine, softened

¾ cup granulated sugar

¾ cup packed dark brown sugar

1 teaspoon vanilla extract

2 large eggs

1 ½ cups mixed nuts (mixed nuts that are available commercially in cans/bags. Do not use honey roasted or smoked

Optional: 1 tub caramel frosting

Preheat oven to 350 degrees. Combine flour, baking soda and salt in small bowl. Beat margarine, granulated sugar, brown sugar, vanilla extract in large mixer bowl until creamy. Add eggs, one at a time, beating well after each addition. Gradually beat in flour mixture. Stir in mixed nuts. Grease a 15 x 10-inch baking sheet. Spread dough into prepared pan. Bake for 20 to 25 minutes or until golden brown. Cool slightly. Cut and continue cooling. If desired glaze with caramel frosting by softening in microwave and drizzling over the top. Enjoy!

Nonpareil Bars

2 ¼ cups all-purpose flour

1 teaspoon baking soda

1 teaspoon salt

1 cup margarine, softened

¾ cup granulated sugar

¾ cup firmly packed light brown sugar

1 teaspoon vanilla extract

2 large eggs

2 cups mini nonpareil candies

Preheat oven to 350 degrees. Combine flour, baking soda and salt in small bowl. Beat margarine, granulated sugar, brown sugar, vanilla extract in large mixer bowl until creamy. Add eggs, one at a time, beating well after each addition. Gradually beat in flour mixture. Stir in nonpareil candies. Grease a 15 x 10-inch baking sheet. Spread dough into prepared pan. Bake for 20 to 25 minutes or until golden brown. Cool slightly. Cut and continue cooling. Enjoy!

Poppy Seed Cookies

½ cup warm water

2 tablespoons poppy seeds

1 cup sugar

1 cup butter

1 egg

2 ½ cups flour

1 teaspoon baking powder

1 tablespoon vanilla extract

extra water

Preheat oven to 375 degrees. Place 2 tablespoons poppy seeds in ½ cup water and allow to soak. Cream sugar and butter. Add egg and beat well. Stir in flour and baking powder. Mix until combined. Drain poppy seeds and add vanilla and poppy seed to the flour mixture. Knead cookie dough, adding extra water if dough is too dry. Form into ball. Wrap and refrigerate for 1 hour. Roll out chilled dough and cut into desired shapes. Place on baking sheet which has not been greased. Bake for 8 to 10 minutes or until golden. Cool. If desired dust with powdered sugar. Enjoy!

Passover Wine Cookies

2 cups vegetable oil
1½ cups granulated sugar
1½ cups white wine
2 pounds passover cake flour
Apricot, strawberry, raspberry preserves

Preheat oven to 350 degrees. Combine all ingredients except for the preserves. Add more cake flour if necessary to allow you to work with the dough. Shape into walnut size balls and place on a cookie sheet which has not been greased. Using the back of a measuring teaspoon make a well in the center of each ball pressing as you do to flatten the cookie just slightly. Fill the wells with preserves. Bake for 25 minutes or until brown. Remove from pan immediately. Cool. Enjoy!

A FISTFUL OF RECIPES

Combinations paying homage to "Alias: Smith and Jones"

We all have our favorite television series. Many of us have gone through several favorites in a lifetime. For decades my top favorite has been a show about two lovable outlaws trying their darnedest to earn an amnesty. Over the years I have written fan fiction to pay tribute and joined discussion groups on social media to meet others who shared my love of the show. Yet, I always wanted something more unusual to pay homage to a show and its characters that brought so much joy into my life. What better way than incorporating it with something I do to bring joy into the lives of others.... creating fun desserts.

I took to a group on social media asking what flavors they thought represented the two main characters. What I have in the next pages are the results of that inquiry. I hope these offerings are a "good deal."

Hadleyburg Bars

2¼ cups all-purpose flour

1 teaspoon baking soda

1 teaspoon salt

1 cup margarine, softened

¾ cup granulated sugar

¾ cup firmly packed light brown sugar

1 teaspoon vanilla extract

2 large eggs

1 10 oz. jar seedless 100% fruit, blackberry fruit spread

Optional: Whole fresh blackberries

Preheat oven to 350 degrees. Combine flour, baking soda and salt in small bowl. Beat margarine, granulated sugar, brown sugar and vanilla extract in large mixer bowl until creamy. Add eggs, one at a time, beating well after each addition. Gradually beat in flour mixture. Grease a 15 x 10-inch baking sheet. Spread dough into prepared pan. Spoon blackberry fruit spread over batter. Use a knife to swirl the fruit spread. Sprinkle whole blackberries on top if desired. Bake for 20 to 25 minutes or until golden brown. Cool slightly. Cut and continue cooling. Enjoy!

Devil's Hole Bars

1 cup margarine, softened

2/3 cup sugar

2/3 cup dark brown sugar

2 eggs

1 teaspoon vanilla

2 cups flour

¾ cup cocoa

1 teaspoon baking soda

½ teaspoon salt

2 cups butterscotch morsels

Preheat oven to 350 degrees.

Cream margarine and sugars. Add the eggs and vanilla. Beat 2 minutes at medium speed. Combine flour, cocoa, baking soda, and salt. Blend into creamed mixture. Stir in butterscotch morsels. Spread mixture into greased 15 x 10-inch baking sheet. Bake for 20 minutes or until tester comes out clean. Cut into squares or rectangles. Enjoy!

Pat Hand Bars

1 cup margarine. softened

2/3 cup sugar

2/3 cup dark brown sugar

2 eggs

1 teaspoon vanilla

2 cups flour

¾ cup cocoa

1 teaspoon baking soda

½ teaspoon salt

2 cups mini chocolate covered mint patties

Preheat oven to 350 degrees.

Cream margarine and sugars. Add the eggs and vanilla. Beat 2 minutes at medium speed. Combine flour, cocoa, baking soda, and salt. Blend into creamed mixture. Stir in mini mint patties. Spread mixture into greased 15 x 10-inch baking sheet. Bake for 20 minutes or until tester comes out clean. Cool before cutting. Enjoy!

Amnesty Bars

2¼ cups all-purpose flour

1 teaspoon baking soda

1 teaspoon salt

1 ½ cups chopped white baking chocolate

¾ cup margarine, softened

¾ cup granulated sugar

¾ cup firmly packed light brown sugar

1 teaspoon vanilla extract

2 large eggs

1 cup chopped pistachio nuts

½ cup semisweet chocolate morsels (optional)

Preheat oven to 350 degrees. Combine flour, baking soda and salt in small bowl. Using your preferred method melt white baking chocolate. Beat margarine, granulated sugar, brown sugar and vanilla extract in large mixer bowl until creamy. Add eggs, one at a time, beating well after each addition. Stir in melted white baking chocolate. Gradually beat in flour mixture. Stir in pistachios. Grease a 15 x 10-inch baking sheet. Spread dough into prepared pan. Bake for 20 to 25 minutes or until golden brown. Cool slightly. Using your preferred method melt semisweet morsels and drizzle over top. Cut and continue cooling. Enjoy!

Story Break

How to Write a Recipe Book in One Hard Lesson

As mentioned in the foreword it was 2003 and I had made the decision to compile some of my more popular/requested recipes into book form. I did not know from "real" self publishing at that time or that it even existed in the way that it does today. What I did know is that I had the basic equipment needed to proceed. I had the hard copies of most of my recipes, my computer's word processing program, the time necessary to work on the project and access to a nearby printing business.

First I decided what categories I was going to have. Next I perused the hard copies of the recipes selecting a combination of the most unusual and the simplest so that people would not be seeing only different versions of things they saw in every other recipe book but there would also be some that I perceived to be things anyone could do and get right.

I chose a word processing program and started formatting pages and entering the recipes. I organized the pages and did a cursory edit. I emailed the pages to a friend who prided herself in her ability to find spelling and grammar errors for a final edit. She returned the file with her assurances that she had "gotten everything". Okay, lesson learned: always check the work of even the most detail oriented person.

I took the files along with a rather primatively designed cover to the printing business, selected the cover color and the type of binding I wanted. Then it was in their hands.

The next day I picked up the proof copy for review, indicated a page adjustment it needed and placed the actual order. Do I have to even mention that they weren't ready when they said they would be? But the day they actually were I arrived to have them tell me that they had accidentally put the binding across the top rather than down the side and was that okay with me or did I want it the way I wanted it. However, many days later I returned to pick up a batch of correctly bound books.

I marketed them myself and was very pleased to have made something happen. I am surprised at this stage in the game that no one ever contacted me over some rather obvious typos and editing gaffs that I discovered to my horror when

I revisited the little book when referencing it while writing "The Great Schmoogle Dessert Book" which I still passed to someone else to check my work. Lesson learned for real this time: check the other person's work and recheck again.

VEGAN, GLUTEN FREE

Spiced Pecan Balls

1 cup gluten free all purpose flour

1 cup finely chopped pecans

3 tablespoons coconut sugar

½ vegan margarine

1 teaspoon vanilla extract

Powdered sugar

Cinnamon (to your preference)

Nutmeg (to your preference)

Preheat oven to 350 degrees. Combine flour, nuts, sugar, margarine and vanilla extract. Mix to form a dough. Refrigerate for 30 minutes. Roll into 1 inch balls and place on parchment lined cookie sheet. Bake for 15 minutes until golden. Remove from oven and cool just to where they are comfortable to handle. While cooling prepare two bowls, one with powdered sugar, the other with a mixture of powdered sugar, cinnamon and nutmeg. While warm roll the balls in the plain powdered sugar. Set aside, then roll in the powdered sugar/spice mixture. Enjoy!

Carrot, Raisin, Walnut Loaf

1 ¾ cup gluten free all purpose flour

2 teaspoon baking powder

½ teaspoon baking soda

¼ teaspoon salt

½ cup coconut oil

¾ cup unsweetened applesauce

1/3 cup coconut sugar

1 heaping cup grated carrot

1/3 cup dark seedless raisins

1/3 cup golden raisins

½ cup finely chopped walnuts

Preheat oven to 350 degrees. Generously grease a nine inch loaf pan. In large bowl combine flour, baking powder, baking soda and salt. In another bowl mix the coconut oil, applesauce and sugar. Mix the coconut oil mixture into the flour mixture and combine well. Fold in the carrots, raisins and walnuts.. Pour into prepared pan and bake for 50-55 minutes or until a tester comes out clean. Cool. Serve warm, room temperature or cold. Enjoy!

Back to Basics Blueberry Pie

2 cups gluten free all purpose (multi purpose) flour

1 teaspoon salt

¾ cup solid coconut oil, chilled

Ice water

4 cups fresh blueberries

½ cup coconut sugar

5 tablespoons gluten free flour

1 tablespoon vegan margarine

Preheat oven to 425 degrees. Combine flour and salt. Cut in the coconut oil until mixture resembles coarse crumbs. Add ice water one tablespoon at a time until dough comes together. Divide in half and roll out each to 1/8 inch thickness. Line 8"or 9" pie pan with one. Toss blueberries with sugar and flour. Fill the pie. Dot with margarine and top with second crust. Seal edges and flute as desired. Cut slits in the top crust. Bake at 425 for 15 minutes. Reduce temperature to 325 degrees and continuing baking for 1 hour or until golden. Cool. Enjoy!

Spiced Peach Cobbler

4 cups sliced canned peaches

¼ cup coconut sugar

½ teaspoon cinnamon (optional)

¼ teaspoon nutmeg (optional)

½ cup melted vegan margarine

½ cup coconut sugar

1 cup gluten free all purpose (multi purpose) flour

1 teaspoon baking powder

1/8 teaspoon salt

Preheat oven to 350 degrees. Brush some of the margarine on the bottom of a 9" x 13" baking pan. Toss the peaches with ¼ cup coconut sugar and spices. Place in bottom of prepared pan. Mix the remaining margarine, 1/2 cup coconut sugar, flour, baking powder and salt. Spoon batter over the peaches. Bake for 25 to 35 minutes or until golden brown. Cool. Serve warm, room temperature or cold. Enjoy!

Harvest Crisp

6 large pears (use your favorite)

¼ cup coconut sugar

1 teaspoon cinnamon

½ teaspoon nutmeg

1 cup dark brown sugar

¾ cup gluten free whole oats

¾ cup gluten free all purpose (multi purpose) flour

½ cup finely chopped walnuts

½ cup cold vegan margarine or coconut oil (if using coconut oil add ¼ teaspoon salt)

Preheat over to 350 degrees. Grease a 9" square pan. Peel, core and cut pears into chunks. Toss with coconut sugar and spices. Place in prepared pan. Combine brown sugar, oats, flour, and nuts. Cut in the margarine or coconut oil. Cover the top of pears with the crumb mixture. Bake for 1 hour. Let stand before serving. Serve warm, room temperature or cold. Enjoy!

Peanut Butter Cookies

2 cups gluten free all purpose (multi purpose) flour

1 teaspoon baking powder

1 teaspoon baking soda

½ teaspoon salt

1½ cups natural chunky peanut butter (no sugar added)

6 tablespoons vegan margarine

1 ½ cups coconut sugar

Egg replacer equivalent to 4 eggs

Preheat oven to 350 degrees. Combine flour, baking powder, baking soda and salt. In a larger bowl mix peanut butter, margarine, sugar and egg replacer. Gradually add flour mixture and combine well. Drop by tablespoonful onto cookie sheets. Use a fork to press down slightly Bake for 10-14 minutes. Cool slightly on cookie sheet. Transfer to rack to continue cooling. Enjoy!

Chocolate Peanut Butter Banana Pop

For anyone who had my original "Just Desserts" book this is the "Ants on a Log" recipe

To make one pop you will need:
1 small ripe banana
Chunky peanut butter
Chocolate shell forming ice cream topping (read labels carefully, some are vegan but some are not)
¼ cup dark seedless raisins (optional)

Split banana lengthwise. Spread sliced sides with peanut butter (press raisins into the peanut butter if desired) Press the sides together. Freeze for 15 minutes. Coat with shell forming topping. Enjoy!

Obligatory Black Bean Brownies

1 ½ cups no salt added canned black beans

¾ cup coconut sugar

1 teaspoon vanilla extract

¼ cup cocoa powder

1/8 teaspoon salt

2 tablespoons vegan margarine

1 teaspoon instant decaf coffee

½ cup chopped walnuts

Preheat oven to 350 degrees. Puree black beans. Add coconut sugar, vanilla, cocoa, salt, margarine and coffee. Mix well. Stir in chopped nuts. Pour batter into greased 8" x 8" baking pan. Bake for 30 minutes. Cool completely. Enjoy!

Obligatory No Bake Cookies

This is a recipe from my original "Just Desserts" book that I converted for this category

½ cup coconut milk

2 cups sugar

3 tablespoons cocoa (you may use raw cacao if you prefer)

½ cup coconut oil

3 tablespoons natural chunky peanut butter (no sugar added)

¼ teaspoon salt

3 cups gluten free long cooking oats

1 teaspoon vanilla extract

In a saucepan combine coconut milk, sugar, cocoa and coconut oil. Bring to a boil. Add peanut butter, salt and oats. Stir until peanut butter is smooth. Boil 1 ½ to 2 minutes stirring often. Remove from heat. Add vanilla. Drop by tablespoonfuls onto wax paper. Allow to cool. Enjoy!

Devil's Advocate Cake

Another adaptation from "Just Desserts" for this category

3 cups gluten free all purpose (multi purpose) flour

2 cups granulated sugar

2 teaspoons baking soda

1 teaspoon baking powder

½ cup cocoa powder

2 teaspoon salt

1 tablespoon cider vinegar

2/3 cup coconut oil, melted

1 teaspoon vanilla extract

½ teaspoon almond extract

1 teaspoon instant decaf coffee (optional)

2 cups cold water

Preheat oven to 350 degrees. Combine all ingredients. Batter will be somewhat loose. Pour into 9" x 13" baking pan that has been greased and floured. Bake for 35 minutes or until tester comes out clean. Frost as desired or serve plain. Enjoy!

CAVALCADE OF CANDY

For every creation you will need:

2 cups morsels
2 cups miniature marshmallows
*1- 2 cups add ins

Use your preferred method to melt the morsels. Stir in marshmallows and listed add ins. Spread on a baking sheet. It will not fill the entire thing and will not be even. Chill for at least 1 hour. Cut into jagged pieces.

*You may wish to vary the amounts of the add ins or use fewer marshmallows depending on your personal preferences. This does not alter the preparation.

Traditional Rocky Road
Semisweet chocolate morsels
1 cup chopped walnuts
Miniature marshmallows

Ode to a Good Bar
Milk chocolate morsels
1½ cups peanuts (not dry roasted)
Miniature marshmallows

S'mores

Milk chocolate morsels

1½ cups graham cracker pieces.

Miniature marshmallows

Sabra

Semisweet chocolate morsels

1½ cups orange jellied candies chopped

Miniature marshmallows

Paradise

White (vanilla) morsels

½ cup shredded coconut

½ cup chopped macadamia nuts

Miniature marshmallows

Ode to Joy

Milk chocolate morsels

½ cup slivered almonds

½ cup shredded coconut

Miniature marshmallows

Baseball Nut

White (vanilla) morsels

1 cup chopped cashews

½ cup chopped dried raspberries

Miniature marshmallows

Ode to Elvis

Peanut butter morsels

2 cups crushed banana chips

Miniature marshmallows

Rose's Butter Brickle Fantasy Candy

Butterscotch morsels

1½ cups toffee bits

Miniature marshmallows

**Chocolate Sprinkles

**note: prepare this as directed above but press the sprinkles on top after spreading onto the pan

Holiday Trio

1. White (vanilla) morsels

1½ cups crush candy cane

Miniature marshmallows

2. White (vanilla) morsels

½ cup chopped walnuts

½ cup chopped cranberry

Miniature marshmallows

3. White (vanilla) morsels

1 cup chopped pistachios

Miniature marshmallows

Afterword

Aside from some of the recipes in the Cavalcade of candy which were newer creations and the recipes in the vegan, gluten free section which I more recently created as well and included so there would be something for everyone the other recipes were those that had been MIA for some time. It had been suggested I title this book "The Lost Recipes" but that would be inaccurate as they are as the title suggests "no longer lost."

Printed in the United States
By Bookmasters